IT'S TIME TO START LIVING.

Understanding how our belief systems fuel addictive behavior

TODD SYLVESTER

IT'S TIME TO START LIVING

Dedicated to my family and friends who never gave up on me.

Published by

Full Circle Partners and Live Academy Publishing
242 E South Temple
Salt Lake City, UT 84111

ISBN 978-0-9978987-5-0

Layout & Design by Scott Windes
and Tanner Capua

"I DIDN'T CHANGE, I JUST WOKE UP."

** BEFORE WE BEGIN **

This information is not meant to be a replacement for medications, in-patient treatment centers, or coaching. Some conditions require immediate attention and should be handled through the appropriate groups and organizations.

For Emergencies - Please use the following resources:

NATIONAL SUICIDE PREVENTION LINE:

1-800-273-TALK

SUBSTANCE ABUSE AND MENTAL HEALTH SERVICES ADMINISTRATION (SAMHSA)

1-800-662-HELP

NATIONAL ALLIANCE ON MENTAL ILLNESS

WWW.NAMI.ORG

ABOUT THE AUTHOR

Todd Sylvester is an experienced motivational speaker and life coach who has spent over a quarter of a century inspiring adults and children alike to avoid and change addictive behaviors. In 1989, Todd founded the non-profit, anti-drug entity Sly Dog, which features the sought-after education program for elementary schools: "Drug Free That's Me." This program has reached thousands of school-age children, emphasizing principles of positive self-talk, personal commitment, goal setting, and character building. Along with school programs, Todd has conducted over 1200 speaking engagements.

Todd currently works as an Addictive Voice Recognition Counselor at a reputable treatment center for those struggling with drug or alcohol addiction, where he provides one-on-one mentoring to both local and international clients. Described as having "a unique gift to develop trusting relationships quickly," Todd has guided hundreds to sobriety and other behavioral successes through the individualized support he offers to each client. His ability to "speak to a person's soul and help them find their true motive to change" has been the key for inspiring others to make permanent lifestyle changes.

INTRODUCTION

YOU SUPPOSE YOU ARE THE TROUBLE.

BUT YOU ARE THE CURE.

- Rumi

I'd like to talk about a new way to view addiction and recovery.

Recently, I sat in a room across from a woman who had been working very hard to overcome her addictions. This woman was my client and at this moment, she was experiencing a breakthrough.

While this breakthrough was wonderful to witness, it wasn't difficult to recognize. For the past 25 years, I had devoted my life to helping others overcome addictions. I'd worked as a speaker, a life-coach, and a clinician. Throughout these years, I had provided countless people with knowledge and tools they could utilize to overcome their addictions. I had witnessed many breakthroughs. I had watched people reclaim their lives from addiction.

A breakthrough is a life-changing moment, filled with an almost immeasurable sense of power and possibility. And yet... it often arrives with a sense of calm and clarity. Because a breakthrough is the discovery of truth. Often, it's the rediscovery of a truth that has merely been forgotten.

Stephanie's breakthrough didn't arrive with any new information. I had simply reminded her of three basic truths that she had always known but – as a result of a lifetime of drug, alcohol, and self-sabotage – had disregarded along the way.

Stephanie left our session inspired by her awareness and newfound motivation to achieve true sobriety. Filled with hope, she shared her experience with a group director at another treatment center… and was promptly scolded. Stephanie's breakthrough did not fit with this program director's view of the world. He refused to accept it and backed that refusal with a master's degree in addiction.

Stephanie returned to me, crushed and confused. She had not even had the opportunity to put her hope into action before an attempt had been made to stomp it out.

I understood Stephanie's pain and sense of helplessness. The truth of my life is that I had spent a great deal of my youth addicted to drugs and alcohol. During this dark period, I disregarded many of the things that were most important to me. I have lived through sadness, self-hatred, and a very real plan to end my own life.

I don't have a master's degree or a Ph.D. I am not classically trained in addiction recovery. But for the past quarter of a century, I have lived a life that is free from drugs and alcohol. I am not a recovering addict. I have recovered. And I have helped others do the same.

Through my experience with both addiction and sobriety, I have discovered truths that, if understood, are the keys to unlocking sobriety, releasing anxiety, and developing a deep, healthy love of one's self.

AND HERE'S SOME MORE TRUTH

"The most powerful weapon on earth is the human soul on fire."

- FERDINAND FOCH -

THIS IS MY STORY

When I was fourteen years old, I fell in love.

It was the first time I smoked marijuana and, for me, it was love at first puff. Smoking pot (or weed, or reefer, or whatever you'd like to call it) brought with it an almost instant feeling of release and freedom... a feeling that I had never experienced before.

That very next Friday night, I got drunk for the first time. To this day, I have no memories of that evening. What I do remember is how painfully my head ached and pounded the following morning. More than that, I remember my friends praising me for being so "crazy" and seemingly confident while intoxicated. Still laughing at the evening that had come before, they told me there was nothing I wouldn't say or do.

From that point forward, I was known to my friends as "Drunk Todd."

I embraced this new persona. And why wouldn't I? My popularity at school was skyrocketing. For the first time in my life, I was considered "cool." In my mind, my exploration into alcohol and other drugs seemed like nothing more than harmless, teenage fun. But in reality, it was slowly taking its grasp on me.

When a few drinks weren't enough, I drank more. When marijuana wasn't enough, I tried harder drugs. When the highs wore off and the lows kicked in, I simply used more alcohol and substances to get those highs back. My life was on a path of addiction and – although those addictions would last almost a decade – I didn't even realize it.

Meanwhile, my life continued forward. By the time I was a senior in high school, I had two obsessions: basketball and partying. I put a lot of time and energy into these obsessions and I convinced myself that I had control over both.

After all, I was a strong basketball player. I worked hard at it. I practiced for hours, every day. I helped win games. When my coach heard rumors about his players indulging in huge partying, I skillfully deflected all suspicion away from me. I was always one step ahead and I felt invincible.

There was only one problem. I was miserable. The initial euphoria I felt by using drugs and alcohol was gradually giving way to depression and an eroding sense of self-worth. When I was using, I felt better. When I wasn't, I felt internal horror and deep pain. I masked that pain with more alcohol and other drugs, which only added anger and sadness.

My seemingly slow path of addiction was now rapidly headed to rock bottom. For me, "rock bottom" was losing my college basketball scholarship mere months after receiving it. I had believed that basketball was everything to me and I now knew that wasn't true. I had sacrificed basketball for addiction and for the first time in my life, I felt worthless.

I was now an "angry drunk," the type of person who punches holes in his own walls. On one especially bad occasion, I even put my head through a wall. I tried everything I could think of to quiet the voice in my head that was telling me that I was worthless, but the only thing that silenced that voice was more drugs.

That voice also told me that there was a way out. And so I planned my suicide.

The plan was simple. The next time I stayed at my parents' house, I would quietly grab my father's shotgun... and I wouldn't have to endure another day of living without worth.

But on the very day that I planned to end my life, something happened. While at school, I overheard a group of girls as they discussed how God could help people in their times of need.

Up until that point in my life, I had never seriously pondered the existence of God or any type of higher power. I had certainly never considered the possibility of reaching for (much less receiving) help from any sort of divine power. But because I believed that I literally had no other hope of recovering my life and self-worth from the clutches of addiction, I knew I had nothing to lose.

AND SO I TURNED **TO A HIGHER POWER**

And for the first time in nearly a decade, I saw a different path... a direction that led to a life that did not revolve around alcohol, drugs, and "partying." The path was long but as I looked ahead, I felt something new. Looking back now, I recognize that feeling as hope. The hope for a better life. A life that was within my reach.

My road to sobriety was not easy. For the first eight months, I couldn't even measure my sobriety with weeks or days. A day was too long, too overwhelming. I measured my sobriety with hours. I didn't want to give up but I was hanging on for dear life, knowing full well that I could slip back into my old life at any moment. What I didn't know is that I was about to experience a breakthrough. Breakthroughs come in all shapes and sizes. On this day, my breakthrough came with a cup of lemonade.

A CUPFUL OF LEMONADE. A HANDFUL OF CHANGE.

I was driving home from work when I passed a little girl's lemonade stand. After stopping and buying a cup, I spontaneously scooped all of the coins that had accumulated in my car's cup holder and gave it to this young entrepreneur. Her face lit up like... well, like a child who had unexpectedly been given a handful of pocket change.

It was such a simple act. I hadn't accomplished anything difficult or noble. I had merely done something small for someone else. And in return... everything inside of me was changing. It was as if a dam that had been holding back a decade of guilt, depression, and sadness had suddenly broken free. Soon, I found myself pulling my car to the side of the road because I was sobbing uncontrollably.

For nearly ten years, my life had been controlled by my addictions. I had felt powerless, a victim of my circumstances. But after making the tiny decision to give this young girl my cup full of change – and seeing the excitement and gratitude that it brought her – I understood that I still had the power to make my own choices – even if, at the moment, they were still small choices.

And for the first time since I had developed my addictions, I began to see that if I stopped focusing on myself and my need for drugs, I could stop the negative thoughts that had been dominating my mind and heart. If I stopped focusing inward – on my own unhappiness and self-centered desire to feed my own addiction – and started focusing on others, I could find true happiness.

RECOVERY

I share my "lemonade story" often because it was so pivotal to my recovery. It was a breakthrough, a catalyst. It wasn't just a moment. This was the moment when everything inside of me began to click into place.

I had the power to choose a different path for myself. I had the power to create feelings of happiness and joy in my life and in the lives of others. I had the power to break free from addiction. I had woken up into my new life and it was a life that made sense.

I began to educate myself on sobriety. I read books written by amazing thinkers, studying the ideas and concepts that I hoped would help me fundamentally rebuild my broken-down sense of self-worth. And I chose to dedicate my life to helping others break free from the chains of addiction and limiting beliefs.

That moment still lives inside of me as if it happened yesterday and yet, it also feels like another lifetime.

I have since worked as a clinician, a life coach, a speaker, and an educator. I have learned much about helping people to sober up – especially those who have struggled in other rehab programs.

I have worked with people who have been to a dozen or more rehab centers all over the nation before ending up in my office as a last resort.

Several years ago, after speaking to a local youth group in my area, I was approached by a film producer to take part in an uplifting video campaign for YouTube. My story, which was told in a short clip entitled "The Hope of God's Light" has been shared and viewed over three million times and translated into three languages.

The popularity of this clip has given me the opportunity to share my message of recovery and change to groups of teenagers and adults all over the country. And although my life's mission is to free people from addictions and prevent young people from ever touching drugs, I have seen – on countless occasions – that the battle with self-hatred and self-loathing doesn't only apply to people suffering through addictions. This is a formula for change that can benefit everyone.

The key to making fundamental, lasting changes in one's belief system is learning to love one's self... truly, absolutely, and completely. This is true for addicts who are trying to get clean, it's true for the person who wants to lose forty pounds, it's true for the child who wants to be better in school, and it's true for the abused spouse seeking the courage to change his or her situation.

By this definition, sobriety equals love of self. And love of self will prove to be the most powerful antidote to addiction or any unwanted behavior.

And yet... learning to love one's self can be a difficult task. Because we all feel the pull of a very destructive force. This force is seldom talked about but it is by far the most dangerous epidemic and malady affecting our society.

This force takes more lives than every drug combined. It destroys homes and tears families apart.

It ruins neighborhoods, corrupts politicians, and drives people to perform evils acts.

When this force possesses an individual, there is almost no limit to what that individual will do to rid themselves of it. We will lie, we will steal, we will eat, drink, and do drugs to excess.

This force is always waiting in the shadows, robbing otherwise good men, women, and children of their dreams. If not combatted, it will poison anyone with feelings of inadequacy and self-loathing. It harms individuals, families, companies, schools, and even entire countries. No one in the world is completely immune from this force. I have seen it live with the rich, the poor, the middle class, the religious, celebrities, business leaders, and the man living in the street. As Benjamin Franklin said:

"Some men die at twenty-five and aren't buried until they are seventy-five."

- BENJAMIN FRANKLIN

This is the force that powers addiction. This is the force that keeps the self-help industry selling billions of dollars of materials every single year. This is the force that keeps drug treatment centers (like the one where I work) filled to capacity year-round.

This force is not a substance. It's not a drug. It's not the media or politics.

This force is an idea.

THE DESTRUCTIVE FORCE — *of* — SELF HATRED

Why is self-hatred so destructive? You might be reading this now and thinking, "I don't hate myself," but that is one of hatred's greatest tricks. It is sneaky. It never comes right out and admits what it is. It shows up in our lives as three basic beliefs that we carry about ourselves.

I am powerless to change, and I will always be the way I am.

I am a victim of my circumstances.

I am broken and "less than."

Typically, these three beliefs arrive mildly... at first. They exist as voices in our heads that whisper to us:

"You're not good enough to do that."

"Who do you think you are?"

In extreme cases, like mine, they'll scream:

"Your soul is damaged and you don't deserve to live anymore."

Every single client that I have ever worked with has been plagued by these beliefs in one form or another. All addictions stem from some variation of these three beliefs. I have yet to come across a single person in any rehabilitation program who has an alcohol or drug problem. All of the people I have met have a belief problem.

The problem with these beliefs... is that people mistake them for the truth.

This feeling of "I am not good enough" or "I am less than" is what fuels addiction to substances, to pornography, to excess spending, or to any other addictive behaviors that produce a "high" – a high that can be used to mask ourselves from these three beliefs. After all, being drunk is a lot easier than having to look in the mirror and face someone we hate.

So where do these beliefs come from? What do these beliefs do to us? And how do these beliefs influence the direction of our lives?

THE BULLY

Every one of us has a voice in our heads. This voice belongs to The Bully.

Have you ever wondered why a celebrity, who appears to possess everything a person could ever desire, is unhappy and addicted to drugs? Or how a wealthy athlete or lottery winner ends up broke in a matter of months or years?

Even with huge changes in someone's external circumstances (such as a large social media following, flashy IMDB profile, or healthy bank account), people will always revert to their old belief system unless it is actively changed. We have all seen examples of people with extraordinary amounts of money, talent, and beauty who still feel, on the inside, like they are ugly, poor, and unqualified.

Why is this? Because The Bully tells us so. The Bully reinforces our negative belief systems. The Bully is the voice in each of our heads that insists:

"I'm not good enough"

"I'm a screw up"

"I'll never amount to anything"

"I'm not smart enough"

And if we break the chains created by The Bully by experiencing some success, The Bully pushes harder:

"I didn't earn that."

"I don't deserve happiness or success."

"I'm a fraud."

"When people find out who I really am, they won't like me."

People living with addictions are well acquainted with The Bully. For example, I remember my Bully telling me:

"I'm a freak."

"I'm too skinny."

"No one likes me."

"I can't be myself unless I'm high or drunk."

And as addiction takes a greater hold on someone (especially after trying and failing, time and again, to clean up), The Bully grows even more intense:

"I'm damaged."

"I'm less than."

"I have a disease."

"I'll never be able to quit using."

"No one would care if I died."

Many of us have heard these voices. Many of us have had these beliefs ingrained into our core essences by The Bully.

The Bully is relentless and strong. The Bully makes it easy for us to loathe ourselves, especially as we work toward sobriety. The Bully pushes us into believing that we are broken.

Our minds believe and obey whatever we tell it, whether we are telling it through our conscious thoughts or our subconscious thoughts (our embedded self-image and belief systems).

So how do we change our self-image?

One of my favorite resources on self-image is "Psychocybernetics," written by Dr. Maxwell Maltz. In his book, Dr. Maltz shares his experiences working as a plastic surgeon in the 1960s. Dr. Maltz had the rare opportunity of seeing people's reactions to their own new, "beautiful" faces and he was often shocked by the immediate boost in self-esteem that many people experienced after surgery.

But what was even more shocking was the number of clients who, after being physically transformed, looked into mirrors and literally failed to see any change in their appearances. They simply continued to feel ugly.

These observations led Dr. Maltz on a lifelong quest to understand the self-image and develop the idea of Psychocybernetics. In his book, he beautifully expresses how The Bully can dictate the outcome of our lives:

"The new science of 'Cybernetics' has furnished us with convincing proof that the so-called 'subconscious mind' is not a mind at all, but a mechanism; a goal-striving mechanism, consisting of the brain and nervous system, which is used by and directed by the mind. "This creative mechanism within you is impersonal. It will work automatically and impersonally to achieve goals of success and happiness, or unhappiness and failure depending upon the goals which you yourself set for it.

"Present 'success goals' and it functions as a 'success mechanism.' Present it with negative goals, and it operates just as impersonally, just as faithfully as a 'Failure Mechanism."

- *Maxwell Maltz, Psychocybernetics, pp. 12-13*

If we allow our minds to be controlled by the voice of The Bully, then we are doomed to lives of misery, addiction, depression, and endless failure. If we can learn to break these chains and silence The Bully, our future happiness, success, and sobriety are literally limitless.

THE BELIEF PRISM

Did you know that research has shown that 77% of the average person's self talk is negative? 77%! That is why we need to pay attention to our self-talk to make sure that our inner voice is positive. Famous sports psychologist Denis Waitley states "Relentless, repetitive self talk is what changes our self-image."

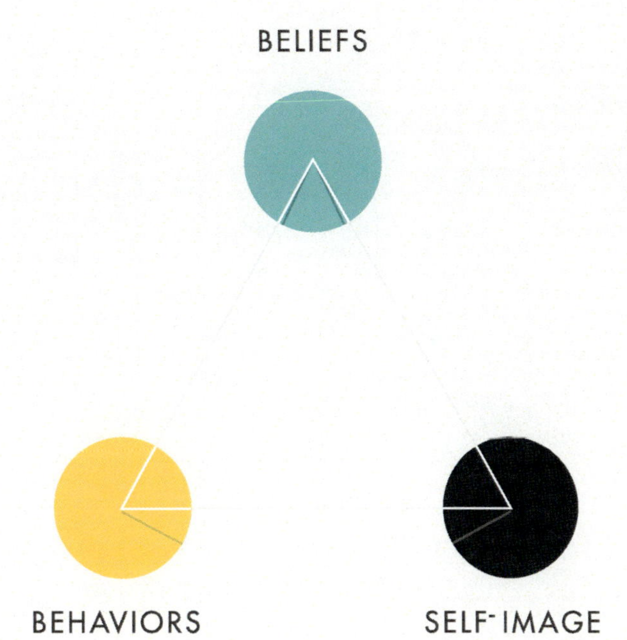

It has been said that the typical individual talks to him or herself approximately 60,000 - 70,000 times each day... and most of the things we say to ourselves are negative.

Consider that for a moment. Now imagine someone going through life with the small, ever-present idea that they are less than another, that they are just not quite good enough. This idea is their self-image. It is their idea of themselves.

At every opportunity, they are reminded that they aren't good enough. When they don't get the job they want, they use that as evidence that they aren't good enough. When they look at social media and see everyone posting photos of all the amazing things they are doing, they feel sorry for themselves and think, "If I were better, then I would have all of these amazing experiences, too."

The evidence solidifies this idea into a belief system. Belief systems are the stories we tell ourselves to define our personal reality.

Belief systems are the sponsors of actions. When we believe that we are "less than," our actions mirror that belief. We carry ourselves as someone who is "less than." We don't look people in the eye when we meet them or give a confident, firm handshake. We hold ourselves back from situations where we can be great because we feel unworthy.

These actions prove to our minds that this belief system is true and they reinforce our self-image. And round and round we go. Self-Image. Belief System. Actions. Validation.

Repetition deepens the impression. Every time these ideas are repeated, the belief system gets stronger and stronger. Every person on earth is subject to the belief prism. The amount of success or failure that any person achieves in life is exactly equal to his or her belief system — without exception.

It's easy to see how our little thoughts about ourselves dictate, and even control, the outcome of our lives.

Gandhi summed it up beautifully when he said:

"YOUR BELIEFS BECOME YOUR THOUGHTS,

YOUR THOUGHTS BECOME YOUR WORDS,

YOUR WORDS BECOME YOUR ACTIONS,

YOUR ACTIONS BECOME YOUR HABITS,

YOUR HABITS BECOME YOUR VALUES,

YOUR VALUES BECOME YOUR DESTINY."

- Gandhi -

"Aerodynamically, the bumblebee shouldn't be able to fly, but the bumblebee doesn't know it, so it goes on flying, anyway."

- MARY KAY ASH

CHANGE YOUR BELIEF SYSTEM, CHANGE YOUR LIFE

When coaching a new client, one of the first things I ask the client to do is read the bumblebee quote.

I ask my clients what this quote has to do with sobriety and the question often stumps them... at first. But after having a moment to ponder this quote, the idea almost always clicks into place, and my clients almost always respond with some variation of the following:

"The bumblebee doesn't believe that it can't fly and therefore, it can."

It's a simple idea – an idea that most of my clients have been unfamiliar with.

Typical recovery programs focus on controlling any and all exterior factors that might have an effect on a person's addictions. The person who is struggling with addictions is labeled as an "addict." This is a label they must live with for the rest of their lives, always reminding them that they are broken.

As "addicts," they are told that recovery is going to be next to impossible – that their chances are "1 in 20." If they do make it through recovery, they must stick to a precise schedule of meetings and maintain absolute and total control over their outside circumstances. Every time I speak with a client who holds these beliefs, I am reminded of how I felt during the first eight months of my sobriety... when I was merely enduring it. When I was "white-knuckling it."

What if we had a different view of recovery and change? What if, instead of labeling someone as an "addict," we reinforced the belief of being clean and absolutely dedicated to sobriety from the inside?

What if we acted like the bumblebee? What would be possible if we only believed that we could fly, instead of focusing on how small our wings are?

I have found the idea of the bumblebee to be the most powerful symbol for my clients in overcoming addiction. My clients that really learn the principle behind why the bumblebee can fly are always able to find a life free from addiction. If you believe that you need alcohol or drugs to get through your day, or you believe that your life is so stressful or painful that you couldn't cope without them, or you believe that your addiction is a disease that you will never get rid of, then you will relapse. You will use again.

Have you ever heard someone say, "I just need my morning coffee so I can get my brain going?" I have, just as I have worked with clients who believe they need to smoke weed or pop an Adderall to be creative. Or others who believe that they need a Red Bull or a Diet Coke to make it through the day.

Recently, a client of mine was getting ready to leave her six-week program. She was doing well but I could sense some hesitation within her. When I asked her about this, she broke down and admitted, "I want this so bad, but I'm really worried about New Year's Eve. I don't think I can have fun without champagne in my hand."

Does this sound familiar?

All of the treatment in the world – any amount of positive thinking, reinforcement, and influence – will have no real power to change a person who fundamentally believes that he or she can't have fun without drugs or alcohol.

I told this client that she may not drink again this coming New Year's Eve or the one after that. But if she allowed that belief to stay with her then The Bully would use it against her. And, without a doubt, she would relapse.

If we want to rid ourselves of addictive behaviors, then we must change our underlying belief systems about those behaviors.

A NEW DEFINITION OF SOBRIETY

The driving power behind changing our limiting beliefs and learning to combat the nagging voice of The Bully comes through learning to love ourselves.

When clients develop a true love for themselves, all the other behaviors dissipate on their own. When clients believe, at their core, that they are good and that they are brilliant, it becomes much easier to say "No" to their particular brand of addiction.

Once we can refuse to accept that we are weak and powerless against The Bully, we can lay the groundwork to develop an empowering new mindset. Through my own experience and through working with thousands of clients, I have learned that the road to lasting sobriety starts with the following premise: We deserve to be loved and we must be willing to love ourselves.

Sobriety no longer means being free of addiction, although that is certainly a part of it. By this definition:

Sobriety is Love of Self.

CREATING

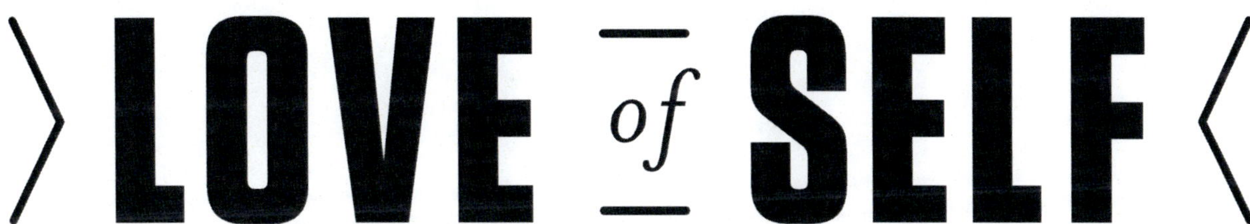

IN OUR LIVES

Like anything else in life, creating a true love of one's self requires practice. It can't happen simply by reading this and won't come merely by attending a seminar or spending time at a rehabilitation center. A fundamental shift in mindset is necessary, as is a willingness to embrace a new set of beliefs and use those beliefs as a guide for life.

I discovered three beliefs through my own recovery and I have watched these beliefs change countless lives. I want you to learn them. I want you to be intimate with them. I want you to believe them at the center of who you are – at your core.

With these positive, affirming beliefs, you can achieve love of self. Read these to yourself often. Memorize them and say them aloud:

I HAVE THE DIGNITY AND ABILITY TO CHOOSE.

I AM A MASTERFUL CREATOR.

I AM POWERFUL BEYOND MEASURE.

If these ideas seem foreign to you, it might be because they are in direct contrast to belief systems people commonly carry. Let's explore, in greater depth, each of these three founding principles.

I HAVE THE DIGNITY AND ABILITY TO CHOOSE

The foundation of any change is the belief that you have the ability to choose. You can change your situation and your circumstances. No matter what state your life is in, you can choose right now, in this very moment, to make it different.

The pull of addiction is very powerful. At least... it can feel that way. Our old ways always pull us in and make us believe that our future is already determined by choices we have made in the past. The truth is that you always have the power and ability to choose, no matter what the circumstances. And this realization is, in itself, a fundamentally empowering truth.

You can choose to be clean and sober today. You can choose to fight back against the voice of The Bully. But remember that what you resist persists. Choose to set yourself apart from The Bully and when you hear his voice... laugh at him!

Consider the words of George Bernard Shaw:

"People are always blaming their circumstances for what they are. I don't believe in circumstances. The people who get on in this world are the people who get up and look for the circumstances they want, and if they can't find them, make them."

I AM A MASTERFUL CREATOR

When we exercise our power and ability to choose, in that moment, we become CREATORS.

When we choose to turn off the TV and engage our minds by reading something positive, we are CREATING feelings of positivity and joy in our lives. When we choose to listen to a small idea like "pull over and give this girl at the lemonade stand all of your change," we are creating feelings of abundance, caring, and happiness.

Everything in our lives – good and bad – was created by US. The law of attraction states that "like attracts like," which means that every time we make a conscious choice, we are ATTRACTING that reality to us. Our mind is a garden. Our thoughts, feelings, and choices are seeds that we plant in that garden. These seeds grow, in our minds, into fully-grown belief systems.

Will we plant an organized, beautiful, and intentional garden? Or will our minds become overrun by weeds and chaos? The choice is ours.

You must learn to separate yourself from the voice of The Bully. When The Bully arrives to declare that you are a powerless victim, you must be able to say to yourself: I am a masterful creator.

Most importantly... you must believe it.

I AM POWERFUL BEYOND MEASURE

As we make positive choices, and we begin to see creations that grow from those choices, we soon see that we are POWERFUL.

As a culture (and especially as “addicts”), we are taught that we are weak and powerless. But when we learn to see the small evidences in our lives, we also learn that we are more powerful than we can even comprehend.

YOU have the power over your own life. You, and you alone, have the power to create the world around you. You can choose to go at the world alone or you can choose to bring good friends into your life and find a connection with a higher power. You don’t have to wait for anyone to rescue you – your inner being holds the power to create anything you want and need.

When you CHOOSE to not listen to The Bully, you CREATE thoughts, feelings, and circumstances that make you POWERFUL.

You are more powerful than your problems. You are more powerful than your addictions!

THE STORY OF TRAVIS

When I first met Travis his outlook on life reflected the classic, self-defeating, powerless archetype.

From a young age, Travis was taught by his father to be honest, polite, and courageous. But when his father left his mother, Travis threw all of these things out the window, declaring them as false and useless. Travis made a decision, from that time forward, to do whatever he wanted to do.

I call this attitude "The Screw-Its." It's a general term that applies to anyone who cares about nothing and no one outside of his or her own self.

Travis began partying at a young age, drinking and smoking pot. All the while, he was building a resentment for his dad, for leaving him and not being an active father after he left. Travis held on to these feelings and so these feelings grew stronger, building up. He never talked about them or dealt with them. Instead, he kept them locked away, in the vault of his mind, like a ticking time-bomb.

Over the years, Travis' addictions evolved. They became stronger. He needed more drugs, substances that worked harder and faster. Eventually, after obtaining a large amount of heroin, Travis was pulled over by a police officer and thrown into jail.

It was in jail where Travis exercised his first little bit of power. He often says that jail only teaches people how to be better criminals – how to get away with more lying, cheating and stealing. He watched as other inmates snorted coffee grounds in a desperate attempt to achieve some kind of high.

At that moment, Travis was disgusted with himself. Being locked in a cell, surrounded by criminals and "addicts," Travis made a simple CHOICE: He didn't want to keep living the way he had. Travis called his mom and asked her to find him a rehabilitation program he could attend once he got out of jail. That's when we met. Travis and I instantly bonded during our first session.

He shared his story with me, I shared mine with him, and he expressed how badly he wanted to change. He told me that my story gave him hope and I told him that true change was not only possible, but could be a reality for him if he was willing to do the work.

We discussed my three foundational principles. I told him that he had the power and dignity to choose something different in his life, that he is a masterful creator and that he is powerful beyond measure. I told Travis that it didn't matter what he had done. He could make it.

During each session, I encouraged Travis to ponder the three principles and to become intimate with their meaning and applicability to his life. The first time I asked him to recite aloud, "I, Travis, am powerful beyond measure," he struggled. Yes, he recited these words back to me, but the words were hollow. It was clear he didn't believe what he was saying.

I presented Travis with a suggestion. I challenged him to recite the phrase 400 times a day. He laughed and said he would try.

But Travis accepted the challenge and took it to heart. For five days straight, he recited "I am powerful beyond measure." Along with it, he wrote a list of all of the positive things about himself. And he made extraordinary progress.

I was overjoyed. Travis' success had affirmed for me that repetition deepens the impression. One day, I asked Travis, "What do you believe about yourself today?"

"I believe I am powerful beyond measure," he replied.

I asked, "Do you love yourself more?"

"Yes!" was his enthusiastic reply.

"Do you have more confidence?"

"Yes!"

"Do you believe you are still damaged?"

"Hell, no!"

Travis' change began with the belief that he could change. And he has embraced the three foundation principles like no one I have ever seen. To this day, Travis still practices the affirmation challenge, every day. "Where I'm at today is, to me, amazing. To be open-minded and to feel clear-headed and to see things I never would've seen when I was using, as to where my life's going... I mean, I'm so positive.

I've learned how to deal with my emotions and not fly off the handle with road rage or little things like that.

Once you realize that these are all things there's nothing you can do about, you really don't have to get all your power taken away from you over something that ticks you off.

And my family life is just amazing because I'm starting to earn trust back with them. Nobody walks on eggshells around me anymore. My life is just... it's awesome. It's hard to explain. Every day is a new day that I'm happy."

- Travis

WHY SELF-LOVE MATTERS

The real goal of sobriety isn't to rid our bodies of harmful substances, but to learn to love and value ourselves so much that we want to end our destructive behaviors.

Unfortunately, addiction – the enemy of self-love – can cause our self-image to deteriorate so completely that we feel unworthy of love, joy, and the company of others. It's a vicious cycle that creates a limiting belief system, a belief that we are irreparably broken and damaged.

No matter what The Bully is telling you, you must separate yourself from that voice and push back. You must create the belief system that you desire, not the one The Bully has been forcing upon you all your life.

The more we can replace our negative belief system with a positive belief system, the closer we get to a radical transformation in our self-image.

Remember... there are only three truths that matter on your road to sobriety:

I have the dignity and ability to choose.

I am a masterful creator.

I am powerful beyond measure.

My approach to sobriety is about learning to train your mind, to condition it to tackle the daily challenge of maintaining sobriety. The techniques I'm advocating are intended to serve as your sobriety self-guarantee.

In other words, this is a guarantee that originates and thrives wholly within you.

My approach will arm you with tools to ensure that your day – this day – remains free of destructive behaviors.

This choice is up to you. Today, you can choose to put this book down and go back to your existing belief systems. Or you can choose, like Travis, to make a different choice.

Is your life where you want it to be?

If it is, I am happy for you. Keep going in the world and make it a better place. If you feel that there is more for you in this life, you can decide and declare – this very day – to be different.

This day, you can love yourself.

THIS DAY, I CHOOSE TO BELIEVE

THIS DAY, I CHOOSE TO WORK

THIS DAY, I CHOOSE TO LOVE MYSELF

THIS DAY, I CHOOSE TO LIVE!

CONCLUSION: IT'S TIME TO START LIVING

As I said at the beginning of this book... I have lived a life that is free from drugs and alcohol for over 25 years. I am not a recovering addict. I have recovered. I have helped others do the same and I can help you.

Sobriety is a lifelong quest toward a healthy, positive, sustainable new belief system. Anyone who suggests that sobriety is possible with less than 100% self-commitment isn't being honest with you.

But there is hope for you. No matter where you may be in your life, you can change where you are going. I did it. I'm doing it. And so can you. If you actively work toward a wholesale remake of your belief system, you can self-guarantee sobriety for the rest of your life.

Start today. Start right now. Recite these affirming beliefs and say them aloud:

1. I have the dignity and ability to choose.

2. I am a masterful creator.

3. I am powerful beyond measure.

THIS DAY, YOU CAN LOVE YOURSELF

"To live is the rarest thing in the world. Most people exist. That is all."

- OSCAR WILDE -

Memorize them. Repeat them, over and over, every day. Say them like you mean them... until you really do. And then, keep going. Learn them. Live them. Believe them.

Re-read this book often. If you know of others who can benefit from the power of self-love, please share this eBook with them.

In 2016, I am publishing the full version of this book. It will be entitled "Sober Up," and it will go into far greater depth about how we can create the belief systems we need to thrive and offer practical techniques and exercises for staying on track through The Seven Daily Principles of Self-Love.

And please know... this book is only the beginning! All the help you need to create self-love is available to you, right now. Visit my website, **toddsylvesterinspires.com**, where you'll find all the information, help, and resources you need to live a life that's free from addiction.

A life of self-love.

IT'S TIME TO START LIVING.

Todd Sylvester

FOR MORE RESOURCES TO HELP YOU WITH YOUR RECOVERY, PLEASE VISIT:

WWW.TODDINSPIRES.COM

FOR LIFE COACHING AND PERSONAL RECOVERY SUPPORT, PLEASE REACH OUT BY CLICKING THE LINK BELOW.

START LIVING

IT'S TIME TO START LIVING.

$7.99
ISBN 978-0-9978987-5-0
50799>
9 780997 898750

Made in United States
Orlando, FL
06 August 2022